VICKIE MILLS

SPACEWAYS

AN ANTHOLOGY OF SPACE POETRY

J O H N   F O S T E R

Illustrations by:
Allan Curless, Peter Elson, Alastair Graham,
Tom Stimpson, and Martin White
Cover Illustration by Julian Baum

D1424147

OXFORD

Oxford University Press, Great Clarendon Street, Oxford OX2 6DP

Oxford New York
Athens Auckland Bangkok Bogota Bombay
Buenos Aires Calcutta Cape Town Dar es Salaam
Delhi Florence Hong Kong Istanbul Karachi
Kuala Lumpur Madras Madrid Melbourne
Mexico City Nairobi Paris Singapore
Taipei Tokyo Toronto

and associated companies in
Berlin Ibadan

Oxford is a trade mark of Oxford University Press

Selection, arrangement and editorial matter
© John Foster 1986

First published 1986
Reprinted 1988, 1991, 1992
Reprinted in paperback with new cover 1997

ISBN 0 19 276068 8 (Paperback)

All rights reserved. No part of this publication may be
reproduced, stored in a retrieval system, or transmitted, in
any form or by any means, without the prior
permission in writing of Oxford University Press.
Within the U.K., exceptions are allowed in respect of
any fair dealing for the purpose of research or private
study, or criticism or review, as permitted under the
Copyright, Designs and Patents Act, 1988, or in the
case of reprographic reproductions in accordance
with the terms of the licences issued by the
Copyright Licensing Agency.
Enquiries concerning reproduction outside these terms
and in other countries should be sent to
the Rights Department, Oxford University Press,
at the address above.

A CIP catalogue record for this book is available
from the British Library

Typeset by Tradespools Ltd, Frome, Somerset
Printed in Hong Kong on the planet Earth

Contents

WATCH THIS
WATCH THIS
WATCH THIS
WATCH THIS
WATCH THIS
WATCH THIS
WATCH THIS
WATCH THIS

Judith Nicholls

S P A C E

P   C

      S P A C E   E
A   S P A C E   M   A
      P A C E   P
      C   T
C   E M P T Y   Y   P

E C A P S

Jenny Thomas

I am ... Star Counting

I am ... lying here counting the stars
that sparkle through my bedroom window.
For years now I've watched them
On winter nights when my eyes grow tired of reading.

So I open the curtain, turn off the light
And tune into the dark.
The stars' light pierces the glass like ice-light
And I start counting.

One ... two ... three ... four ... plus three on Orion's belt ...

By the time my eyes close for sleep
I'm already at eleventyteen thousillion ...

It's too dark to write it down,
Not to worry, I'll start again tomorrow night.

John Rice

Davy by Starlight

Climbing rung after rung the scrambling-
    net of the skies,
Over roof-top and quayside crane
    went Davy's eyes.

They glinted in primitive wonder
    with starlight thrown
From suns that cooled a million years
    before he was born.

And rung after painful rung, his slow
    thoughts climbed the night –
Cat-walking roof and chimney-pot
    at a dizzying height –
Till they slipped and were tumbled headlong
    into strange seas of light!

Raymond Wilson

Technicians

The geometry of sky
  extends its angles. Look,
beyond the hemisphere
  of pen and book
sharp points of light appear
  as if a tall
compass were turning there.
  Stars beyond call
or counting, answer to
  its measurements,
going — man knows not where,
  nor, coming — whence.

But who can quantify
  the algebra of space,
or weigh those worlds, that swim
  each in its place?
Who can outdo the dark?
  And what computer knows
how beauty comes to birth —
  shell, star and rose?

Jean Kenward

Stars

They present light as evidence of the past;
Their brightness reaches us from another time:
They were there when the earth was waste,
When life slithered out of humid slime.

They were there to keep concepts in sight,
To hold a pattern as a path above
The darkness, to be the guiding light
When men walked upright, saw them, fell in love.

Alan Bold

Sky Seasons

The most magnificent of sights
on chilly winter nights
is to see Orion
show his power and glory.

And in summer's bright dawn
just as day is being drawn
you'll hear Venus
tell her age-old story.

It's in autumn and spring
when our sky season king
the Great Bear
writes the world's long history.

John Rice

12

Andromeda

On a mole-black night when the stars are bright
And the cloud-veiled moon is high,
If you search near the wings of Pegasus
You can see her in the sky.

Chained fast to a rock, she waits her fate
As the great sea-monster's prey;
As she hides in fear she can hear the hiss
Of Cetus on his way.

But wait, it's the swish of Pegasus' wings
With Perseus riding high!
On a mole-black night with the stars in flight
You can see them ride away.

Judith Nicholls

Make Believe

When I wake up in the morning
Not all is what it seems
I drift through a world of make believe
Between my real life and my dreams.

Strange adventures from the Space book
That I read the night before
Crowd in upon my drowsiness
Through imagination's door.

Between sleeping and waking
The alarm clock's jangling cry
Becomes the roaring fire-tailed rocket
That hurls me through the sky.

My bed's a silver space craft
Which I pilot all alone
Whisp'ring through endless stratospheres
Towards planets still unknown.

Outside through the mists of morning
The spinning lights of cars
In my make-believe space voyage
Become eternities of stars.

Is that my mother calling something
That my dreams can't understand?
Or can it be crackling instructions
From far off Mission Command?

14

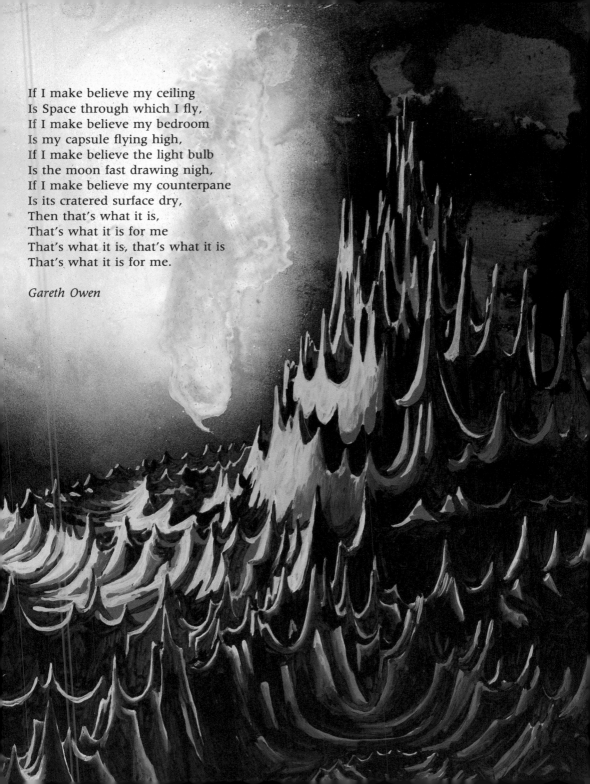

If I make believe my ceiling
Is Space through which I fly,
If I make believe my bedroom
Is my capsule flying high,
If I make believe the light bulb
Is the moon fast drawing nigh,
If I make believe my counterpane
Is its cratered surface dry,
Then that's what it is,
That's what it is for me
That's what it is, that's what it is
That's what it is for me.

Gareth Owen

Shed in Space

My Grandad Lewis
On my mother's side,
Had two ambitions.
One was to take first prize
For shallots at the village show,
And the second
Was to be a space commander.
Every Tuesday
After I'd got their messages,
He'd lead me with a wink
To his garden shed
And there, amongst the linseed
And the sacks of peat and horse manure
He'd light his pipe
And settle in his deck chair.
His old eyes on the blue and distant
That no one else could see,
He'd ask,
'Are we A O.K. for lift off?'
Gripping the handles of the lawn mower
I'd reply:
'A O.K.'
And then
Facing the workbench,
In front of shelves of paint and creosote
And racks of glistening chisels,
He'd talk to Mission Control.
'Five-Four-Three-Two-One-Zero-
We have lift off.
This is Grandad Lewis talking,
Do you read me?
Britain's first space shed
Is rising majestically into orbit
From its launch pad
In the allotments
In Lakey Lane.'

And so we'd fly,
Through timeless afternoons
'Till tea time came,
Amongst the planets
And mysterious suns,
While the world
Receded like a dream:
Grandad never won
That prize for shallots,
But as the captain
Of an intergalactic shed
There was no one to touch him.

Gareth Owen

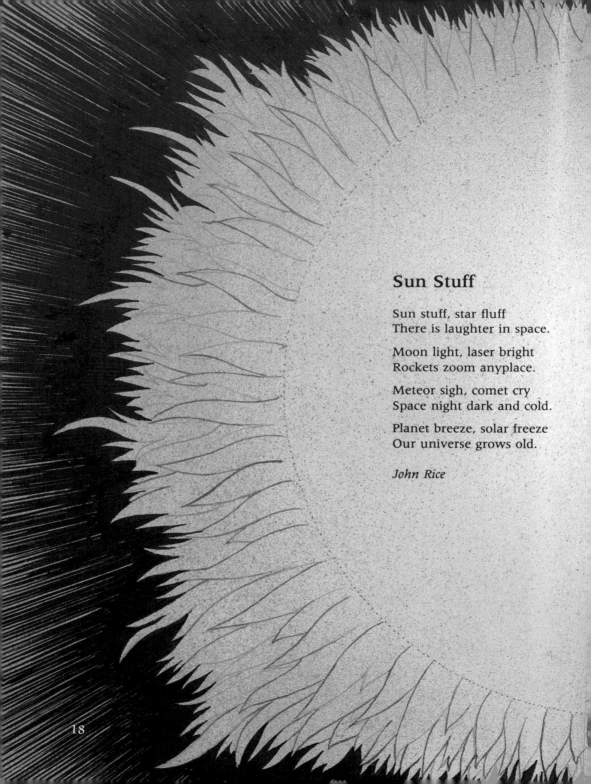

Sun Stuff

Sun stuff, star fluff
There is laughter in space.

Moon light, laser bright
Rockets zoom anyplace.

Meteor sigh, comet cry
Space night dark and cold.

Planet breeze, solar freeze
Our universe grows old.

John Rice

Sun

You travel swiftly
    with a single purpose.
Despair or joy
    can make no difference –
alter your pace,
    persuade you to regress,
or cool the quivering surface
    of your face.

You carry gold,
    yet sometimes come in silver,
or pewter-coloured,
    feathered with bright flame
bird-like ... a phoenix ...
    or a sunflower.
The sightless feel you.
    Children know your name.

You are as old, it seems,
    or aeons older
than that through whose parameter
    you pass;
are called a god, a fire,
    a star, a symbol,
or Light itself, ghost visible
    through glass.

Jean Kenward

Moon

At its fullest the moon
Looks like a sadly exposed clown

Beaming at a captive audience who are
Patiently waiting for the real star:

Sleepy, slothful, soulless creatures
Staring at the blandest features –

A round zero, a nothing of a face
Mooning around the wastes of space.

Alan Bold

Moon

Sometimes fat
  sometimes thin,
sometimes like
  a lemon skin;
sometimes pale,
  sometimes bright,
in the first hour
  of the night
followed by
  a single star,
secret
  as a jaguar. . . .

Sometimes faint,
  sometimes lit:
who could have
  suspended it
far beyond
  our earth and air?
How was it
  established there
with a gold
  and silver skin,
sometimes fat –
  sometimes thin?

Jean Kenward

Moon

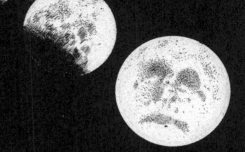

Never the same,
she spills her liquid silver
nightly,
or, like a miser keeping gold,
hides behind cloud.
The sun is her supporter
while it is dark:
from him her strength is gathered,
and so she moves
supremely as a swan.

Later, the early onslaught of the lark
jostles her out of power.
She becomes
a spectral moon
fragile as rice paper:
no longer that magnificent tycoon
swollen and proud –
now, at the gaze of noon
her flesh falls from her, meekly.
She is gone.

Jean Kenward

To the New Moon

In the beginning God created the heaven
and the earth, and in due time
set moon and stars in the heavens;
and on the seventh day he rested.

After a thousand ages, man,
made in his image and likeness,
without ever resting, with his
lay intelligence
one October night, without fear,
set in the tranquil heavens
other bodies like those
that had been spinning
since the creation of the world. Amen.

Quasimodo   *translated by Jack Bevan*

Astronauts

Brown earth, blue,
  pale blue
   receding

Grey-white moon
in a sky of black

Earth again, home
  in a flaming spear
   to dusk-fire:

Fire to fire
and back
to water.
   The earth trembles.

John Travers Moore

23

Count Down

A ten wolf pack
On a nine tree hill
Howls eight notes
That shiver the seven skins of man
And make him try to kill
By counting
The six hours to dawn
On his five-fingered hands,
Whilst four legs scuttle
From the skill of the howl
To the three-dimensional dark
Of a hole
Watched by two measuring eyes
Of an owl.
So the one moon
Is hunted down the round sky.
Night, wolves and moon
Are over the hill,
By and gone.
The count down is done.
The sun
Rockets into sight,
Begins its climb
In giddy light
As ten birds sing
On a nine tree hill . . .

Julie Holder

Brokendown Countdown

Tense	Nice	Ates	Sonce	Sykes	Fice	Force

A
THE L UNCH

```
                    o
                   wo
                  be n
                  utni
                  kyla
                 tronau
                 acefli
                 acecra
                nvention
                e believ
                l be wor
                 million
                 nks will
                 abilitat
                 geniuse
                 seconds
                 nce will
                 e needed
                 cience F
                 l come t
         In ten sec nds' time
             New    rds
             Will   eeded
              Sp    k
               S    b
               As   t
              Sp    ght
              Sp    ft
               I    s
          No on        ed in
             Wil       th
              A
             Cra       be
             Reh       ed
             As        s
         In ten        ' time
             Scie      do
         What onc         magic
         And S           iction
             Wil         rue.
```

Stanley Cook

Thrice   Twice   Once   NONCE!

John Rice

Space Shot

Out of the furnace
The great fish rose
Its silver tail on fire
But with a slowness
Like something sorry
To be rid of earth.
The boiling mountains
Of snow white cloud
Searched for a space to go into
And the ground thundered
With a roar
That set tea cups
Rattling in a kitchen
Twenty miles away.
Across the blue it arched
Milk bottle white
But shimmering in the haze.
And the watchers by the fence
Held tinted glass against their eyes
And wondered at what man could do
To make so large a thing
To fly so far and free.
While the unknown Universe waited;
For waiting
Was what it had always been good at.

Gareth Owen

The Eagle has Landed

The airlock swings open –
behold! a new world:
obsidian black sky
lit by the sun's
fierce glare.
Inch
down the ladder –
the first man on the moon!
Look!
The first footprint.
Listen!
The first word
splitting the still dead silence.
Dead dust
dead rock
dead black sky.
A dead dead world.
Zombie in a moontrance I
trip
stumble
fall
rise
before the slow dust settles.
I leap in lingering arches.
Steady yourself.
Get your samples –
moondust moonrock.
Temperature check.
Humidity test.
And so
plod
carefully back.
My footprints in the ancient dust.

Adrian Rumble

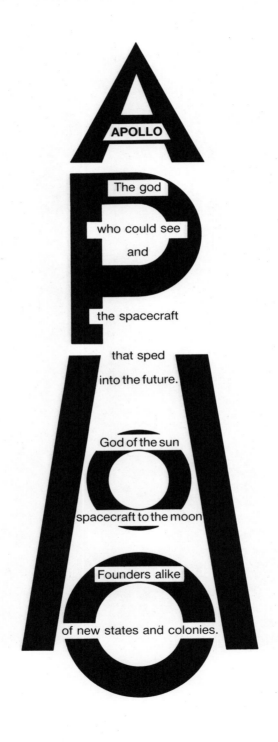

APOLLO

The god

who could see

and

the spacecraft

that sped

into the future.

God of the sun

spacecraft to the moon

Founders alike

of new states and colonies.

Stanley Cook

28

Stanley Cook

Moonscape

No air, no mist, no man, no beast.
No water flows from her Sea of Showers,
no trees, no flowers fringe her Lake of Dreams.
No grass grows or clouds shroud her high hills
or deep deserts. No whale blows in her dry
                                    Ocean of Storms.

Judith Nicholls

Dog-watch

Black velvet flecked with silver points
Where no day breaks the light and dark
Nor hour from hour; where the cold
Brings no winter and no winter cold

Among the swirling dust where no wind blows
Nor brings the rain to new spring plants
Wrapped in the heavy clouds from under which
We sent a piece of home
For a few men to see an earthrise from the moon.

Neil Harries

Earthset

Night spreads like purple heather
over wasteland sky
and marbled earth rolls gently into sleep.

Earthrise

Earth rises blue above the ragged grey;
night horses draw dark cloud away
and earth again rolls into shining day.

Judith Nicholls

31

Space Trip

We three climbed the ever-narrowing
spiral, the pitblack orbit
into a funnel of space
to cull, out on a limb of stars,
that mistletoe cluster, the sacred
deadwhite nothing of the moon.
Blank as a meteorological balloon,
at the very sight
of us it froze with fright.

We found the prospect harrowing
but clambered out, eyed the lunatic
horizon, on sprung-heeled boots
bounced about a bit, grubbed rocks, played golf.
– Then zeroed in on the return funnel, bright
as moonday, though not quite.
We climbed that orbit, too,
out of the crater of the view

into the spiral ever-narrowing
towards that better nothing – O so round,
so various, so living. And so blue!

James Kirkup

Aldrin Collins and Armstrong

```
5
4
3
2
1  ROCKET
2  THE MOON
3  FLEW IT
WHAT 4  ?
5
4
3
2
```

Michael Rosen

The space race! The space race!
What has it all been for?
Stockpiling satellites
To wage a nuclear war?

The space race! The space race!
Wouldn't it have been more worth
Spending all that money
To improve life on Earth?

Derek Stuart

Man and Height

At times the success of a mission
was indescribable.
Fortunately there were few deaths,
though one would wonder
at those fuel-burst explosions
at take-off.

The landings were so complex —
a million intricate mechanisms
that could backfire or an ill-timed
break in the electrics.

7.7 million pounds of thrust
pushing Apollo 16 up into
the speechless oceans of space.

Its exhaust plume disappeared
about 4 to 5 miles up, and
turning from the television
I saw my baby son achieving
a record 5 building bricks high.

John Rice

Song In Space

When man first flew beyond the sky
He looked back into the world's blue eye.
Man said: What makes your eye so blue?
Earth said: The tears in the ocean do.
Why are the seas so full of tears?
Because I've wept so many thousand years.
Why do you weep as you dance through space?
Because I am the Mother of the Human Race.

Adrian Mitchell

Space Settlement

My father was one of the first men
Who mined the moon for materials
(How I loved to say their names when
I was young – aluminium, titanium,
Iron, silicon) to make gigantic
Tubular wheels that weightlessly
For ever float revolving gently
In the vastness of space.

When I was ten,
My family came to live in this space
Settlement. What joy, what unbridled pride
My parents felt to be among those chosen
To be the sole saviours of the human race,
Supplying it with solar energy, essential,
As its precious stocks of oil and coal ran out.
My only brother and I, we did not doubt
We would be happy here.

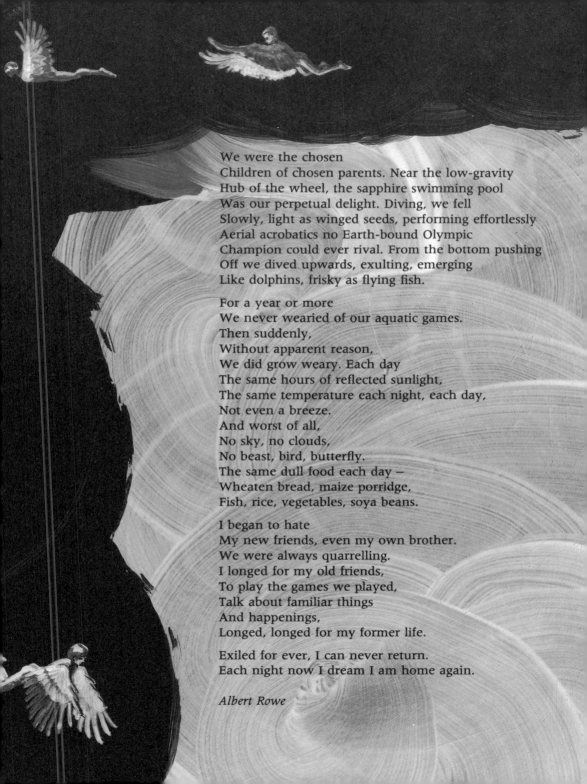

We were the chosen
Children of chosen parents. Near the low-gravity
Hub of the wheel, the sapphire swimming pool
Was our perpetual delight. Diving, we fell
Slowly, light as winged seeds, performing effortlessly
Aerial acrobatics no Earth-bound Olympic
Champion could ever rival. From the bottom pushing
Off we dived upwards, exulting, emerging
Like dolphins, frisky as flying fish.

For a year or more
We never wearied of our aquatic games.
Then suddenly,
Without apparent reason,
We did grow weary. Each day
The same hours of reflected sunlight,
The same temperature each night, each day,
Not even a breeze.
And worst of all,
No sky, no clouds,
No beast, bird, butterfly.
The same dull food each day —
Wheaten bread, maize porridge,
Fish, rice, vegetables, soya beans.

I began to hate
My new friends, even my own brother.
We were always quarrelling.
I longed for my old friends,
To play the games we played,
Talk about familiar things
And happenings,
Longed, longed for my former life.

Exiled for ever, I can never return.
Each night now I dream I am home again.

Albert Rowe

The Ballad of Morgan the Moon

The Americans claim they were the first to land on the moon. This song argues differently and tells the story of that pioneering pipe fitter, Morgan Jones, who was known throughout the valley as 'Morgan the Moon.'

Old Mog the mechanic, I remember him well.
He once built a rocket, or so they will tell,
From an old winding-engine he found on the dole,
Built in the Rhondda and powered by coal.

And when it was finished he painted it red,
And he called it *Bethania*, or so it is said.
And he took it up a mountain on a night late in June
'To get that bit closer,' said Morgan the Moon.

Sleepy Treorchy was bathed in white light
When the shuddering hulk took off in the night.
A deafening scream and then a great roar,
And up past the houses old Morgan did go.

His heat-shield was glowing like anthracite coal
And we prayed down in Cardiff, in mission control.
The barrow-wheels dropped as was previously planned
And old Morgan prepared for *Bethania* to land.

He landed like linen on a crusty old crater:
Dai said he'd get there lunar or later!
So off Morgan went in the moon's swirling dust,
To collect some rock samples from a crater's hard crust.

A strange piece of rock soon old Morgan found,
Just lying there shining on the dust-covered ground.
He picked it up closely and he let out a call
'Cos written right through it in Welsh was 'Porthcawl'!

Max Boyce

39

Moon-wind

There is no wind on the moon at all
    Yet things get blown about.
In utter utter stillness
    Your candle shivers out.

In utter utter stillness
    A giant marquee
Booms and flounders past you
    Like a swan at sea.

In utter utter stillness
    While you stand in the street
A squall of hens and cabbages
    Knocks you off your feet.

In utter utter stillness
    While you stand agog
A tearing twisting sheet of pond
    Clouts you with a frog.

A camp of caravans suddenly
    Squawks and takes off.
A ferris wheel bounds along the skyline
    Like a somersaulting giraffe.

Roots and foundations, nails and screws,
    Nothing can hold fast,
Nothing can resist the moon's
    Dead-still blast.

Ted Hughes

Moon-transport

Some people on the moon are so idle
They will not so much as saunter much less sidle.

But if they cannot bear to walk, or try,
How do they get to the places where they lie?

They gather together, as people do for a bus.
'All aboard, whoever's coming with us.'

Then they climb on to each other till they are all
Clinging in one enormous human ball.

Then they roll, and so, without lifting their feet,
Progress quite successfully down the street.

Ted Hughes

'Jump over the moon?' the cow declared

'Jump over the moon?' the cow declared,
  'With a dish and spoon. Not me.
I need a suit and a rocket ship
  And filmed by the BBC.

'I want a roomy capsule stall
  For when I blast away,
And an astronaut as a dairymaid
  And a bale of meadow hay.'

She gave a twitch of her lazy rump,
  'Space travel takes up time.
I certainly don't intend to jump
  For a mad old nursery rhyme.'

Max Fatchen

Here is the News from space

The Space News Agency Atmos report
that the sun can be seen quite a lot
these days,
but not very much
at night.

The spokesman in the moon said:
'Hey diddle diddle
the cat and the fiddle
the cow jumped over the moon.
The little dog laughed
to see such fun
and the dish ran away with the spoon.'

Venus police have issued identikit pictures
of the cat and the cow, and
a dish is being held for questioning.
Police have put out a special appeal
for any little dog at or near the moon
at the time
to come forward and help with further investigation
of the affair.

Michael Rosen

Humpty Dumpty went to the moon

Humpty Dumpty went to the moon
on a supersonic spoon
He took some porridge and a tent
but when he landed
the spoon got bent.
Humpty said he didn't care
and for all I know
he's still up there.

Michael Rosen

The Owl and the Astronaut

The owl and the astronaut sailed through space
In their intergalactic ship
They kept hunger at bay
With three pills a day
And drank through a protein drip.
The owl dreamed of mince
And slices of quince
And remarked how life had gone flat
'It may be all right
To go faster than light
But I preferred the boat and the cat.'

Gareth Owen

44

Space Spot

Twinkle, twinkle little star
  Up there in the blue.
How I wonder what you are,
  Are you Dr Who?

Max Fatchen

45

Rockets and Quasars

Rockets and quasars
Planets and stars.
I'm fed up with Earth
So I'll see you on Mars.

John Rice

The Children

Who built the canals on Mars?
No one knows.

And who planted the rose
on Jupiter?

I think it must have been children
jumping from star to star
with their silvery parachutes
playing a game of their own.

Iain Crichton Smith

MARS

SPACE-SHUTTLE

Monday
my Aunt Esmeralda
gave me one of those
s p a c e - h o p p e r s.
You know,
those big orange things
that you sit on and
they're supposed to take you to the stars.
Didn't take me any further than
the lamp-post —
and that hurt.

Tuesday
I gave it to my baby brother.
Do you know, he really believes
it's going to work!
Some people will believe
anything.

Friday.
Just had a postcard
from my brother.
From the moon.

It says
'Had a good journey.
See you soon.
Just hopping off to Mars!'

Judith Nicholls

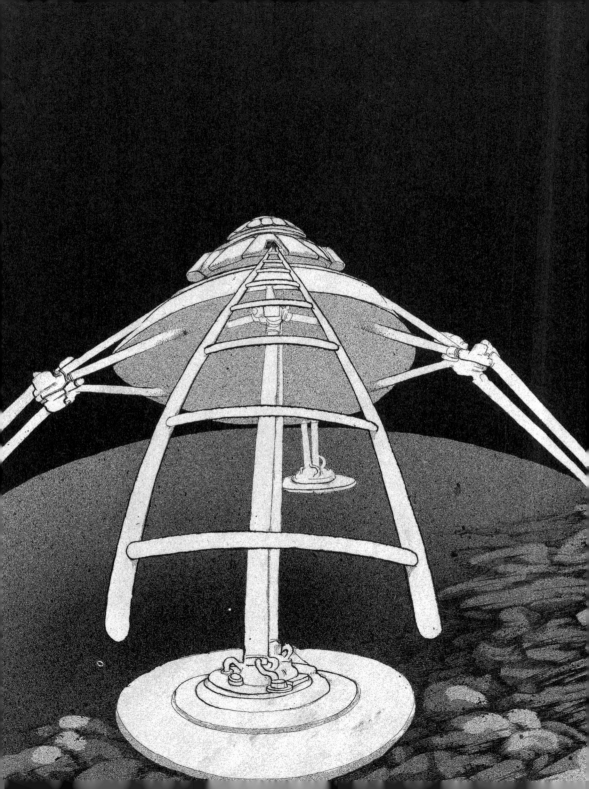

Sci-fi Horrorscopes

1   At Martian dawn
     In fireproof boots
     Trepid explorers
     Pussy-foot
     Round the lip
     Of the mouth
     Of the tepid volcano
     Hoping it won't wake up
     And yawn.

2   Proudly he stepped
     Out onto the new planet
     And his booted foot
     Dissolved.

3   Like a sharp attack of fear,
     The dexterous control-column
     Gripped his stomach.

4   'Come back inside!'
     I yelled to my twin.
     But she was snatched up
     By the rubber midwife.

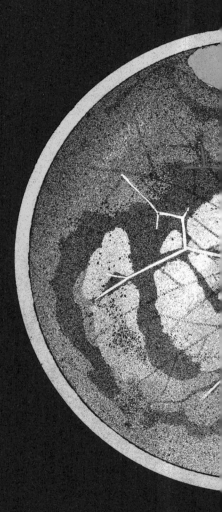

5 As I went to shake him by the hand –
   Congratulations, a successful mission –
   It turned to jelly.

6 'Are you there?'
   'Where?'
   'Down there!'
   'I am.'
   'Who are you?'
   'I've no idea!'

7 Fumbling desperately, madly,
   Finally he managed to jerk his knife
   From its protective scabbard
   And gasped to see it neatly slice
   Through his oxygen-pipe.

8 Every night and all night
   Earthly nightmares
   Mar Mars.

9 One, two,
   Buckle my toe.
   Three, four,
   It fitted before.
   Five, six,
   You're in a fix.
   Seven, eight,
   What a fate!
   Nine, ten:
   To have to learn to walk again.

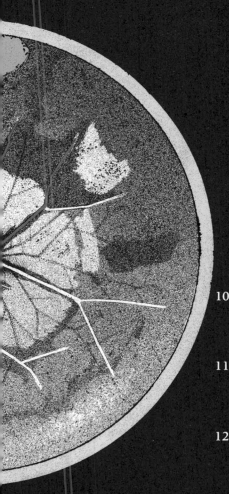

10 If only I could walk, or even crawl,
    I could get some food from the ship.
    Then I could have a meal,
    If only Ed hadn't borrowed my stomach.

11 'What can you see through the telescope?'
    'Red rivers crossing a white landscape.'
    'So his eyes are very bloodshot.
    He's old, so we may escape!'

12 'Why bring all that junk into the ship?
    You know it's very crowded!'
    'But I want to bring some souvenirs
    Of dear old Mother Earth.'
    'But why on earth — why, in heaven's name?'
    'Because I enjoyed my time there.
    Besides, it's being demolished next week.'

Geoffrey Summerfield

The First Men on Mercury

— We come in peace from the third planet.
Would you take us to your leader?

— Bawr stretter! Bawr. Bawr. Stretterhawl?

— This is a little plastic model
of the solar system, with working parts.
You are here and we are there and we
are now here with you, is this clear?

— Gawl horrop. Bawr. Abawrhannahanna!

— Where we come from is blue and white
with brown, you see we call the brown
here 'land', the blue is 'sea', and the white
is 'clouds' over land and sea, we live
on the surface of the brown land,
all round is sea and clouds. We are 'men'.
Men come —

— Glawp men! Gawrbenner menko. Menhawl?

— Men come in peace from the third planet
which we call 'earth'. We are earthmen.
Take us earthmen to your leader.

— Thmen? Thmen? Bawr. Bawrhossop.
Yuleeda tan hanna. Harrabost yuleeda.

— I am the yuleeda. You see my hands,
we carry no banner, we come in peace.
The spaceways are all stretterhawn.

— Glawn peacemen all horrabhanna tantko!
Tan come at'mstrossop. Glawp yuleeda!

— Atoms are peacegawl in our harraban.
Menbat worrabost from tan hannahanna.

— You men we know bawrhossoptant. Bawr.
We know yuleeda. Go strawg backspetter quick.

— We cantantabawr, tantingko backspetter now!

— Banghapper now! Yes, third planet back.
Yuleeda will go back blue, white, brown
nowhanna! There is no more talk.

– Gawl han fasthapper?

– No. You must go back to your planet.
Go back in peace, take what you have gained
but quickly.

– Stretterworra gawl, gawl . . .

– Of course, but nothing is ever the same,
now is it? You'll remember Mercury.

Edwin Morgan

Last Men on Mars

The earth shook, stumbled, shuddered,
It was all over in an hour or so.
Some men on Mars looked out,
Stared at the glow in the starry sky
As if nothing had happened,
Got on with their delving,
Carried out instructions.
Back home everything went to pieces,
Structures that had endured
Majestically fell flat.
Pyramids, skyscrapers, columns:
They all fell down.
The streets were sticky with blood and vomit,
It was all so messy like
The end of everything.
The honorary Martians, not much wiser,
Finished what they had come to do,
Packed up and took off
Leaving gleaming instruments shining behind.
So radio contact had cut out.
So what; they could cope with a fault,
Were programmed to keep cool.
They kept cool.
Their carrier left the Martian soil
Arching gracefully out of orbit
Then thrust towards the familiar little planet.
It was as bright as a beacon.
They had done their job,
Home was on the horizon.
Their craft carried on
Like a thrown stone.

Alan Bold

Our Solar System

We made a model of the Solar System today
On our school field after lunch.
Sir chose nine of us
To be planets
And he parked the rest of the class
In the middle of the field
In a thoroughly messy bunch.
'You're the sun,' he brays,
'Big, huge; stick your arms out
In all directions
To show the sun's rays.'
The bit about sticking arms out
Really wasn't very wise
And I don't mind telling you
A few fingers and elbows
Got stuck in a few eyes.
Big Bill took a poke at Tony
And only narrowly missed him,
And altogether it looked
More like a shambles
Than the start of the Solar System.
The nine of us who were planets
Didn't get a lot of fun:
I was Mercury and I stood
Like a Charlie
Nearest of all to the sun,
And all the sun crowd
Blew raspberries and shouted,
'This is the one we'll roast!
We're going to scorch you up, Titch,
You'll be like a black slice of toast!'
Katy was Venus and Val was Earth
And Neville Stephens was Mars,
And the sun kids shouted and
Wanted to know
Could he spare them any of his Bars.
A big gap then to Jupiter (Jayne)
And a bigger one still to Saturn,
And Sir's excited and rambling on
About the System's mighty pattern.

'Now, a walloping space to Uranus,' he bawls,
'It's quite a bike ride away from the sun.'
Ha blooming ha — at least somebody here's
Having a load of fun.
He's got two planet kids left
And Karen's moaning
About having to walk so far:
She's Neptune — I suppose Sir's
Cracking some joke about
Doing X million miles by car.
Pete's Pluto — 'The farthest flung of all,'
Says Sir,
He's put by the hedge and rests,
But soon he starts picking blackberries
And poking at old birds' nests.
'Of course,' yells Sir, 'the scale's not right
But it'll give you
A rough idea.
Now, when I blow my whistle
I want you all to start on your orbits —
Clear?'
Well, it wasn't of course,
And most of the class, well,
Their hearts weren't really in it,
Still, Sir's O.K. so we gave it a go,
With me popping round the sun
About ten times a minute,
And Pluto on the hedge ambling round
Fit to finish his orbit next year.
We'd still have been there but
A kid came out of the school and yelled,
'The bell's gone and the school bus's here!'
Well, the Solar System
Broke up pretty fast,
And my bus money had gone from my sock
And I had to borrow.
I suppose we'll have to draw diagrams
And write about it tomorrow.

Eric Finney

Planets

Mercury, Venus,
Jupiter —
older than us all
you are:
older than the bird
that sits
bursting its emphatic
wits
in a battery
of song.
Long, have you existed ...
long ...

Longer than the time
that locks
ammonites
into the rocks ...
longer than
the dragonfly
who emerges
but to die.
Longer than
the snowflake's flight —
cropped and vanished
in a night.

Beautiful you are,
austere
with the strength
that holds you there,
each obedient
to his place
in the boundless
roads of space ...
serpentine
as quicksilver —
Mercury, Venus,
Jupiter.

Jean Kenward

60

The planets turn in stately dance

The planets turn in stately dance
Around the sun. Venus, Saturn,
Mercury and Mars, Uranus,
Neptune, Pluto, Jupiter and Earth –
Lit by the sun, they run
Their measured course. The stars
In startling order roll around
The stars – lit too by stars.

It's so much more (and less)
Than all the twinkle twinkle
Of my nursery-rhyming days.
And I grow older just as puzzled
Now as then about their birth.
Upholstered astronaut, I hear
The spinning music of each sphere
And never cease to be amazed.

John Kitching

The Tenth Planet

There was this buoyant blue balloon
That felt a little spare.
It had been given life on Earth,
Was puffed with human air.

It bumped into a telescope
And glanced at outer space;
It thought it saw some more balloons
Each with a friendly face.

It gazed on all the planets
That lay beyond the moon:
Mars, Jupiter, Saturn,
Uranus and Neptune.

And further out was Pluto,
A cold and distant sphere;
That had to be the target,
The loneliest by far.

So the balloon floated upwards,
Sneaked through the Earth's thick clouds;
Saw stars above get closer
And, down below, the crowds.

The Earth itself got smaller,
A mottled ball of blue;
It too was balloon-like
From a certain point of view.

Out, out into the darkness
The balloon kept to its course.
It kept away from comets
Speeding among the stars.

Mars was red and arid,
Jupiter was gas,
Saturn's rings were brilliant,
Uranus a great mass.

Neptune was a freezeup
And - furthest out of all -
Pluto, the ninth planet,
A revolving snowball.

Past Pluto was a dark spot
Where a planet ought to be;
The balloon took its position
To orbit endlessly.

Back on Earth astronomers
Studied evidence
Of a new, tenth planet
And called it Providence.

They say they'll send a spaceprobe
To Providence quite soon;
They'll either find some sign of life
Or burst their own balloon.

Alan Bold

What's Out There?

What's out there?
I wish I knew.
Maybe someone
just like you?
Maybe someone
who's like me?
People . . . people
I can't see?

What's out there?
Do voices call
softly
far beyond us all?
Somewhere –
on some planet's hem –
wait for us
to answer them?

What's out there?
An eye, which looks
into different
picture books?
Has a different
language – sees
different mountains,
different trees?

Can there be
another race
spinning round
in outer space –
wondering
about us, too?
What's out there?
I wish I knew.

Jean Kenward

Within the space

Within the space,
Between the space,
Beyond the space,
Through starry lace,
Another race,
A kinder face,
A gentler grace.

John Kitching

My Thing from Outer Space

I dreamed I was a Thing from space
without a home, without a face.

I had no hair, I had no head
but a hundred eyes all blazing red.

I had no toes, I had no skin
and I was neither fat nor thin.

My bones were made of bright green jelly,
and my mouth was in my belly.

I could not walk, but like a top
kept spinning round without a stop.

It was a problem, never knowing
if I was coming or was going.

I had no front and no behind.
I was most curiously designed.

And when I took a bath, I swear
I felt that I was soaping air . . .

It was the weirdest dream I dreamed:
it was more real than it seemed!

But then I vanished out of sight
and woke up in the dead of night

myself again, at home, in bed,
with arms and legs and face and head,

my mouth no longer in my belly,
my bones no longer made of jelly,

with toes and fingers, skin and hair,
my front and behind no longer air.

— But for a long time there I lay
awake, till night had turned to day,

and tossed and turned, still wondering
if I had dreamed I was a Thing

or if that Thing from space could be
dreaming it had changed to me.

James Kirkup

A Close Encounter

I was returning from a friend's one night
when our street was bathed in a ghostly light
and an eerie drone filled the air.

My trembling hand clutched the gate, and there –
in the middle of the road – large and round
was a shining object touching down.

It shimmered and glowed as if alive;
made a humming and buzzing as if a hive
of bees was swarming inside.

Well, I tell you this and I swear it's no lie;
a trapdoor opened, a ladder swung down
and a strange looking creature wobbled down to the ground.

Its huge nodding head was a great bulbous dome.
It had one staring eye in a forehead of chrome
and it was looking straight at me!

Then it lifted up its lobster claw
and beckoned me gently to its door,
slowly shifting its grasshopper legs.

It had no mouth but it made a noise
which must have come from a hidden voice.
Its electric crackle plainly said:

'We have come from Mars the planet red.
We offer peace and friendship to every man.
You are welcome to visit our land, if you can.

Step inside, earthling. Do not be afraid.
We have ideas to exchange and thoughts to trade.
There is much to be learnt from each other.'

Though I knew the words he spoke were true,
I was much too frightened to know what to do.
So I fled up the path to our house.

A welcoming light, and my mum making toast.
'What on earth can be wrong?' said my dad.
'Have you just seen a ghost?'

Adrian Rumble

Questions and Answers (a ballad)

Momma dear, and Poppa dear,
Tell me, please, how I came here.

   From no-time, from no-place.
   You came, dear child, from outer space.

But Momma dear, and Poppa dear,
Your answer fills my heart with fear!
What is no-time, what is no-place,
And what and where is outer space?

   These are all questions, without doubt,
   You need not worry your head about.
   When you are older, then, my dear,
   We'll tell you just how you came here.

I'm old enough to know right now
Just when I was born, and where, and how.
I want to know the facts, the truth —
I'll soon have grown into a youth —
So Momma dear, and Poppa dear,
Tell me, please, how I came here.

   Well, dearest child, we'll let you know
   How you came here on earth below.
   You came from Saturn, Jupiter or Mars,
   From Venus, or those undiscovered stars
   So far away, their light has not
   Yet reached this blessed plot
   Lost in the silver seas of dark
   Like a tiny flying spark.
   Or from some immense black hole
   You were punted into goal.

Oh, Momma dear, and Poppa dear,
What was the hour, day and year?

    No diary recorded it.
    No calendar recorded it.
    No quartz chronometer recorded it.
    No horoscope gave word of it.
    No Advanced Warning System ever heard of it.

Was there no sign,
No computer put on line?
Did I not show up bright green
On some memory-bank's grey screen?

    It was not shown on any clock,
    For like a faint electric shock
    Or minor earthquake, you
    Arrived out of the blue
    That is so black, so utterly unknown,
    Far beyond the shining bone
    The new moon hangs up in the sky,
    Beyond all reach of mortal eye ...

So now I know how I came here –
More or less – my parents dear.
But will you kindly tell me now
Why I came to you, and more precisely how?

You came here in a rocket ship
That landed on the rubbish tip
Beside the gasworks, where they pile
The trash and refuse, mile on mile
Of software, hardware, all the junk
The earthlings scrapped when they did a bunk –
To intergalactic colonies, we think –
And left us others on the brink
On this disintegrating earth
Where only robots now give birth.
But we really do not know why 'they'
Sent you to us that winter day.
But who are 'they'? Where do they live,
And do they often have to give
Children like me, and let them grow
With strangers whom they do not know?

   We do not know who 'they' may be,
   Nor do they really know what we
   Might feel – if pain or grace –
   At being sent a child from space.

Then Momma dear, and Poppa dear,
Tell me, when I go from here,
Where shall I fly, and tell me, pray,
What must I do to find my way
With my teddy, with my cat
To wherever 'they' will aim me at?

   – Back to the darkness you shall go,
   Dear, darling child, from here below.
   A flying saucer will alight
   And take you off into the night
   Of space, so infinite, so far,
   And drop you on some distant star
   Where you shall soon forget your mystic birth
   And all you know of life on earth.

But – will you also join me there
In the cold and empty air
Of nothingness – In that black hole, will you stay near,
My Momma dear, my Poppa dear?

  No. Our answer, dear, is no and No.
  Alone, all all alone you'll go
  Out into wastes of endless black,
  And never never once look back
  To wave goodbye to wave goodbye
  As you vanish vanish vanish in the sky.

  While we two, left here cold as stone,
  All alone and all alone,
  Gaze up beyond the moon's white bone
  To watch your little flying spark
  Dying away into outer dark –
  Dying away, dying away, dying away into outer dark . . .

But I'll come back –
They'll let me come back, won't they?
Momma dear, and Poppa dear – please say
They will – Don't let me die –
I'll come back one day – won't I?
Come back – I will –
O, let me – let me come back – still
Come back – to you – to you – to you . . .

James Kirkup

Four Children, One Being.
Four Children, One Seeing.

The small ship
Came down in the garden
Hardly disturbing the night.
The Being stepped out
As it landed,
Walking upright.
Its fur was like frost
In the moonshine
Sparkling with light.
It was as tall as I
No more—
It looked into my eyes
And knew me sure as sure.
I wanted to show that I liked it,
I wanted to smile—
I tried—
But it set no store
By anything I knew—
I cried...

No No!
The ship was huge—
The Alien too
But it had no form—
Like fog it was
You could see right through
Eyes it had, I think,
That floated round inside it.
Like diamonds they were,
Faceted and prism'd
That surely denied it
Any sight as we see,
The coldness of it
Was space grown
It wasn't anything that could be known
Or could know me
It turned the colour of things to grey.
I was terrified—
I ran away!

Not at all!
The ship was small
But did not touch the ground.
The thing rolled out sounding laughter
And bounced around.
It shot out a sort of hand
And showed me in the palm
Stars and planets wheeling.
I thought it meant no harm
Though it whirled around and round me,
Dizzied me and sent me reeling —
I thought it was playing.
It showed me toys and treasure and keys,
Come — come with these, it said,
In no voice that I heard
But I saw that it shrank
From touching trees
And I said, without word—
I'm staying.

I was watching from the window.
What made you act so weird?
Why did you cry
And run
And stare
As though you saw something
                        you feared?

Were you playing a game?
Or did something give you a
                            scare?

I watched from the window
All the time —
And I saw nothing there!

Julie Holder

75

Supposing

A sinister spacecraft came down on the field,
And a hatch in the saucer slid back and revealed –
A nightmare of Martians, all grey and green streaks,
And they each had three legs and three eyes and three beaks!
Then, wobbling weirdly, one came right across
And in Martian demanded to speak to the boss.
So we led him in school, to the headmaster's door,
And we knocked, and he opened, and then when he saw –
His eyeballs fell out with a plop on the floor!

Eric Finney

Space Joke?

'Knock knock' said the Astronaut.
'Who's there?' said the Alien.
'A Human Being' said the Astronaut.
'A Human being what?' said the Alien.

Julie Holder

The Marrog

My desk's at the back of the class
  And nobody, nobody knows
    I'm a Marrog from Mars
With a body of brass
    And seventeen fingers and toes.

Wouldn't they shriek if they knew
  I've three eyes at the back of my head
    And my hair is bright purple
My nose is deep blue
    And my teeth are half-yellow, half-red.

My five arms are silver and spiked
  With knives on them sharper than spears
I could go back right now if I liked –
  And return in a million light-years.
I could gobble them all,
For I'm seven foot tall
  And I'm breathing green flames from my ears.

Wouldn't they yell if they knew,
  If they guessed that a Marrog was here?
Ha-ha, they haven't a clue –
  Or wouldn't they tremble with fear!
  'Look, look, a Marrog!'
  They'd all scream – and SMACK
The blackboard would fall and the ceiling would crack
  And teacher would faint, I suppose,
But I grin to myself, sitting right at the back
  And nobody, nobody knows.

R. C. Scriven

77

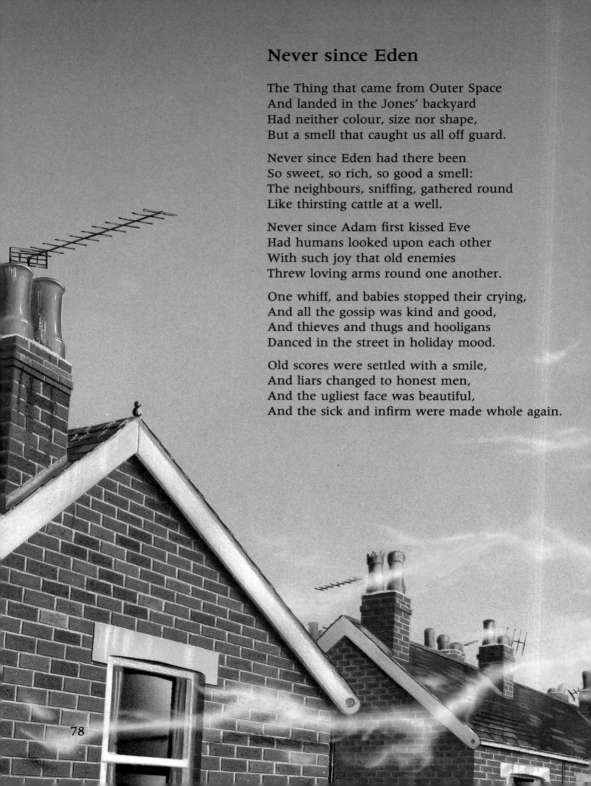

Never since Eden

The Thing that came from Outer Space
And landed in the Jones' backyard
Had neither colour, size nor shape,
But a smell that caught us all off guard.

Never since Eden had there been
So sweet, so rich, so good a smell:
The neighbours, sniffing, gathered round
Like thirsting cattle at a well.

Never since Adam first kissed Eve
Had humans looked upon each other
With such joy that old enemies
Threw loving arms round one another.

One whiff, and babies stopped their crying,
And all the gossip was kind and good,
And thieves and thugs and hooligans
Danced in the street in holiday mood.

Old scores were settled with a smile,
And liars changed to honest men,
And the ugliest face was beautiful,
And the sick and infirm were made whole again.

The Thing that came from Outer Space
Purred like a cat at the heart of the smell,
But *how* it did, and *why* it did,
Was more than the Scientists could tell.

They roped it off, they cleared the streets,
They closed upon it, wearing masks,
Ringed it with geiger-counters, scooped
And sealed it in aseptic flasks.

They took it back to analyse
In laboratories white and bare,
And they proved with burette and chromatograph
That nothing whatever was there.

They sterilized the Jones' backyard
(The smell whimpered and died without trace),
Then they showed by mathematics that no Thing
Could have landed from Outer Space.

So the neighbours are quite their old selves now,
As loving as vipers or stoats,
Cheating and lying and waiting their chance
To leap at each others' throats.

Raymond Wilson

Message Understood

The Scantext stutters
'ALERT' in my brain.
I await further instructions.
The message comes through.
'SOLUTION CONCERNING THE ROBOTS.'
This has been expected.
I await further instructions.
My personal robot tries to read
The message in my brain
But my hypocrisy defeats him.
He smiles back at my false smile.
In many ways he is almost human.
The message is absorbed.
'THE ROBOTS HAVE OUTLIVED THEIR USE.
THEIR AMBITION THREATENS US.'
I await further instructions.
'LAST WEEK THREE OF THEM
WERE SEEN DANCING AND SINGING
IN THE DESERTED BALLROOM.'
I await further instructions.
'IF EACH HUMAN PLAYS HIS PART
THEN NO ONE WILL BE GUILTY.'
Message understood.
I prime my hand laser.
My robot turns to me
With something in his face
That in a man you might call fear.
For three seconds I squeeze the trigger.
The fine rod of light penetrates him.
He falls to the ground
His eyes turning to water.
Something like a song
Invades his throat
And his mouth leaks red.
Soon the threat will be over
If all humans do their duty.
Humming to myself
I await further instructions.

Gareth Owen

Strangers

Strange one, who are you
with your face like a cartoon
red horns on your head
and your lips like a rainbow?

You are like no one I ever saw
standing there,
such a strange visitor
at my ordinary door.

And yet I welcome you
as I see you thinking,
Who is this strange one
with the fur on top of a bowl?

Iain Crichton Smith

The Undistinguished Visitor

'But I'm nothing unusual,' he said.
'My life is utterly undistinguished.
I've invented nothing, composed no symphonies,
Designed no temples, bridges or palaces.
Until today I've hardly travelled –
Only to planets less than twenty light-years distant,'
Said the anthropoid with scarlet fur and telescopic eyes,
Who could hear a bat squeak from a mile away,
Outcalculate our largest computer,
And run forty miles in an hour on his seven-toed feet.
'To be frank,' he continued, 'they chose me
As being especially stupid,
And therefore suitable for leaving behind from the real expedition
To investigate this planet of yours
Which we call Garbage-Bucket.'

Leo Aylen

Phew

On the floor of the universe
in a dark corner
where cosmic dust gathers,
mushrooms grow.

Though edible,
they are difficult to pick
because of their size.

In fact, they are so big
that it would take all the people
who ever lived on planet Earth
a million billion zillion light years
to eat even half a one for breakfast.

Also just think:
All that butter. Phew.

Roger McGough

The Fungus Fingers

where the icebergs break in splinters
where the glaciers melt and flow
where the snow is deep as houses
    there the fungus fingers go

where the lightning rips the sky-cloth
where the sunburst blinds your eye
where the rain dissolves high mountains
    there the fungus fingers fly

where the islands drown in oceans
where the monsters growl and bawl
where the forests shake with anger
    there the fungus fingers crawl

where the Space Police are wide-eyed
where the skulls dry in the sun
where the laser beams split planets
    there the fungus fingers run

where the echoes boom through valleys
where the ghostly shadows creep
where the night falls like a hammer
    there the fungus fingers LEAP!

Wes Magee

85

Alien goes Shopping

He went into the shop and sat down.
'Can I help you?' asked the girl,
trying not to notice his rainbow eyes,
his one green spiral curl.

'Shoes. Eight,' he said. She brought
a shiny brown pair. 'Much too wide,
too long, and not enough of them,'
he cried; and then he threw aside

his cloak and showed her his four pairs
of shoeless feet, with claws bright blue
and nicely trimmed. 'Certainly, sir,' she said
and measured them. Four pairs. Size two.

Pamela Gillilan

Alien at the Zoo

The monkeys looked from their cages
and saw him, with his many-coloured eyes
and high green curl, dressed in a long
cloak, grey as winter skies.

They knew he wasn't a man.
'Be like us,' they called. 'Leap and swing,
throw off your grey cloak.' And he did!
He began to jump and spring

and run faster than horses can
on his eight legs. But the people ran away.
They thought he was the most gigantic
spider in the world. The zoo was shut all day.

Pamela Gillilan

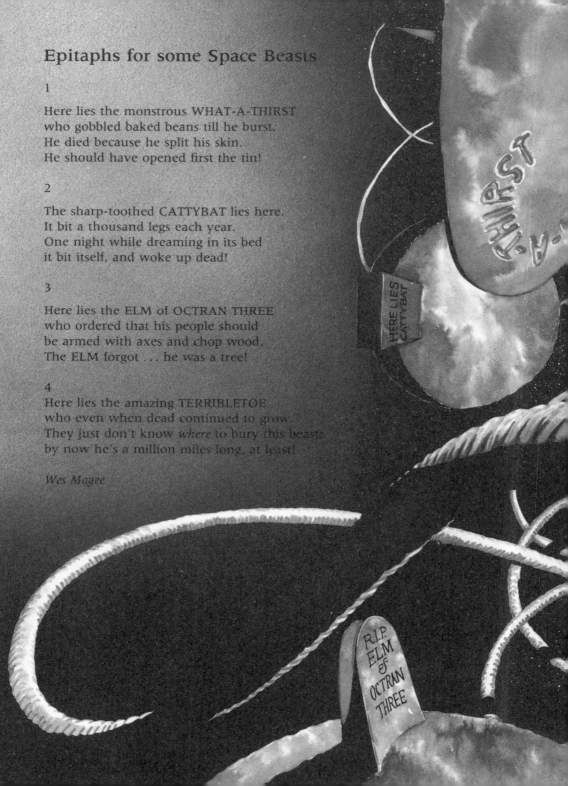

Epitaphs for some Space Beasts

1

Here lies the monstrous WHAT-A-THIRST
who gobbled baked beans till he burst.
He died because he split his skin.
He should have opened first the tin!

2

The sharp-toothed CATTYBAT lies here.
It bit a thousand legs each year.
One night while dreaming in its bed
it bit itself, and woke up dead!

3

Here lies the ELM of OCTRAN THREE
who ordered that his people should
be armed with axes and chop wood.
The ELM forgot ... he was a tree!

4

Here lies the amazing TERRIBLETOE
who even when dead continued to grow.
They just don't know *where* to bury this beast:
by now he's a million miles long, at least!

Wes Magee

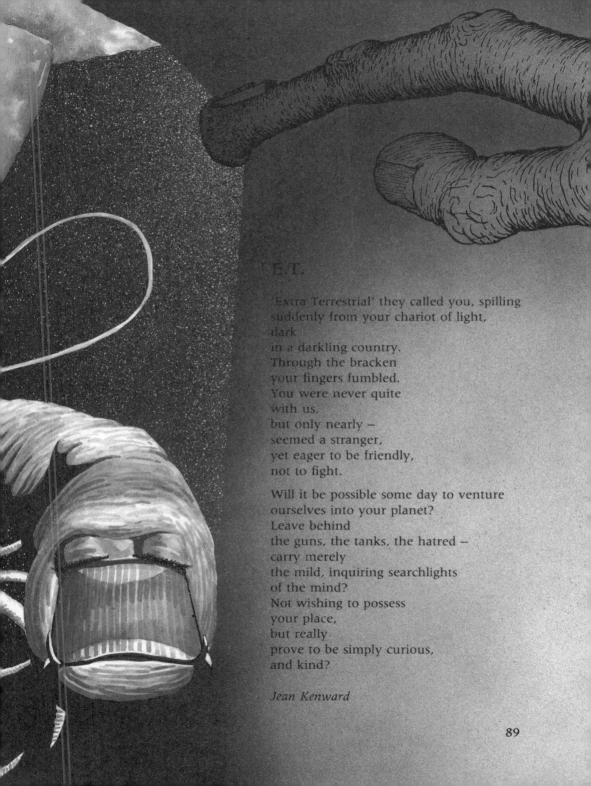

E.T.

'Extra Terrestrial' they called you, spilling
suddenly from your chariot of light,
dark
in a darkling country.
Through the bracken
your fingers fumbled.
You were never quite
with us,
but only nearly —
seemed a stranger,
yet eager to be friendly,
not to fight.

Will it be possible some day to venture
ourselves into your planet?
Leave behind
the guns, the tanks, the hatred —
carry merely
the mild, inquiring searchlights
of the mind?
Not wishing to possess
your place,
but really
prove to be simply curious,
and kind?

Jean Kenward

I know where I'm going

I know where I'm going.
I don't know who's going with me.
I know the muffled whispers
In the air. But are there unknown ears
That hear my silent song?

John Kitching

Unique?

How strange
to think
that somewhere
out in deepest space,
millions of years away,
there is
someone
who is just
like me.

Yet stranger still
to think
that nowhere
in all those
vast dark worlds
is there
anyone
who could be
like me.

Adrian Rumble

On Some Other Planet

On some other planet
near some other star,
there's a music-loving alien
who has a green estate car.

On some other planet
on some far distant world,
there's a bright sunny garden
where a cat lies curled.

On some other planet
a trillion miles away,
there are parks and beaches
where the young aliens play.

On some other planet
in another time zone,
there are intelligent beings
who feel very much alone.

On some other planet
one that we can't see,
there must be one person
who's a duplicate of me.

John Rice

Off to Outer Space Tomorrow Morning

You can start the Count Down, you can take a last look;
You can pass me my helmet from its plastic hook;
You can cross out my name in the telephone book –
    For I'm off to Outer Space tomorrow morning.

There won't be any calendar, there won't be any clock;
Daylight will be on the switch and winter under lock.
I'll doze when I'm sleepy and wake without a knock –
    For I'm off to Outer Space tomorrow morning.

I'll be writing no letters; I'll be posting no mail.
For with nobody to visit me and not a friend in hail,
In solit'ry confinement as complete as any gaol
    I'll be off to Outer Space tomorrow morning.

When my capsule door is sealed and my space-flight has begun,
With the teacups circling round me like the planets round the sun,
I'll be centre of my gravity, a universe of one,
    Setting off to Outer Space tomorrow morning.

You can watch on television and follow from afar,
Tracking through your telescope my upward shooting star,
But you needn't think I'll give a damn for you or what you are
    When I'm off to Outer Space tomorrow morning.

And when the rockets thrust me on my trans-galactic hop,
With twenty hundred light-years before the first stop,
Then you and every soul on earth can go and blow your top –
For I'm off to Outer Space tomorrow morning.

Norman Nicholson

The craft I left in was called Esau

The craft I left in was called Esau,
at least that name was scratched on the smooth door
I went in by. Someone said the engineers
gave them all names, I don't know. The stars
outside were what I noticed first; they looked
so incongruously normal. People joked
nervously; just like a plane flight.
They found seats, wondered if bags would fit,
gestured at the stars and told each other:
'Be seeing those in close-up soon'. No bother,
no big deal. I can't recall feeling sad,
not then. I think I was too interested
in the achievement, the technicalities.
And when we took off, there were the night skies
ahead; still, so still, a new ocean.
It seemed natural to look for an horizon,
as a captain would look where he was bound,
not back to port. Then the ship turned,
just slightly, and there was our long bright wake
already closing, and we looked back
along it to where you could still trace
charted coastlines on the bluish mass,
quite small really; uncanny with distance,
our late guesthouse; our inheritance.

93

Sheenagh Pugh

Space Men

Ten fearless Space Men orbiting in line;
A meteor hit one and then there were nine.

Nine happy Moon-Landers danced to celebrate;
One dropped into a crater and then there were eight.

Eight hopeful Space Men soared straight up to heaven;
Only one got past the gates and then there were seven.

Seven foolish Space Men, flying blind for kicks;
One joined a different galaxy and then there were six.

Six cruising Space Men, eager to arrive;
One opened up the hatch too soon and then there were five.

Of five Mars-landed Space Men one was such a bore;
The rest cut off his oxygen and then there were four.

Four returning Space Men should have landed in the sea;
One came down in Moscow and then there were three.

Three reluctant Space Men didn't have a clue;
One fell in the fuel tank and then there were two.

Two hungry Space Men, their food had almost gone;
One ate all the other's share and soon there was one.

One stupid Space Man in orbit round the sun
Thought his mission was a landing, so then there was none.

Charles Connell

The Space Explorer's Story

Having locked ourselves
airtight in the capsule cockpit,
having checked precisely
that all the instruments said
'GO!'

We flew
beyond the pull of gravity
beyond our own imaginations
deeper into space,

tons of it swirled around us
filled up to the brim with darkness
and absolutely nothing more.

After several years
of exhaustive exploration
and many detailed surveys
of large meteors and planets
we discovered that we were

spinning round and round in blackness
totally alone.

David Harmer

Spacepoem 3: Off Course

the golden flood   the weightless seat
the cabin song   the pitch black
the growing beard   the floating crumb
the shining rendezvous   the orbit wisecrack
the hot spacesuit   the smuggled mouth-organ
the imaginary somersault   the visionary sunrise
the turning continents   the space debris
the golden lifeline   the space walk
the crawling deltas   the camera moon
the pitch velvet   the rough sleep
the crackling headphone   the space silence
the turning earth   the lifeline continents
the cabin sunrise   the hot flood
the shining spacesuit   the growing moon
   the crackling somersault   the smuggled orbit
   the rough moon   the visionary rendezvous
   the weightless headphone   the cabin debris
   the floating lifeline   the pitch sleep
   the crawling camera   the turning silence
   the space crumb   the crackling beard
   the orbit mouth-organ   the floating song

Edwin Morgan

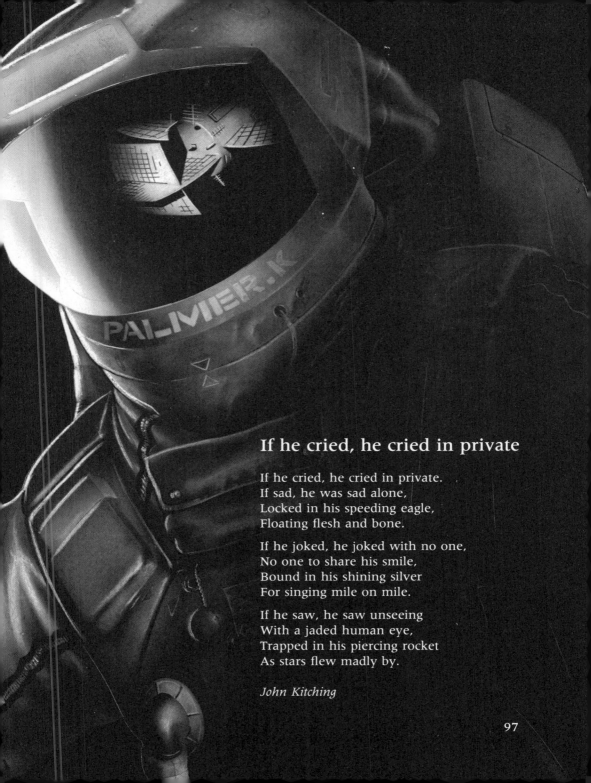

If he cried, he cried in private

If he cried, he cried in private.
If sad, he was sad alone,
Locked in his speeding eagle,
Floating flesh and bone.

If he joked, he joked with no one,
No one to share his smile,
Bound in his shining silver
For singing mile on mile.

If he saw, he saw unseeing
With a jaded human eye,
Trapped in his piercing rocket
As stars flew madly by.

John Kitching

Save Our Spaceship

When you're far beyond the solar system
In the vast depths of outer space
And your oxygen supply is running low;
When you have fired off your final missiles
At the closing alien crafts;
When you are at the mercy of the foe.

When your main computer circuit's broken
And you've lost contact with Earth;
When you're hurtling straight towards a black hole;
When your craft's disintegrating slowly;
When the fuel tank's nearly empty
And the capsule's spinning out of control.

When your plight is really desperate;
When you've almost given up hope;
There is only one thing left for you to do.
You must send out the special signal
That only Timelords can decode.
Someone (Guess Who!) will come to rescue you.

Derek Stuart

Scale = 1·0

—18
—17
—16
—15
—14
—13
—12
—11
—10
— 9
— 8
— 7
— 6
— 5
— 4
—3
— 2
— 1

8
7
6
5
4
3
2
1
0
1
2
3

EMERGENCY

GRAVITY ANOMALY
HIGH POTENTIAL
01 G to ∞ < ·7 AU

Ship = ✳ G level 9·5
Thrust = → G level 9·0

Scale = 0·

Black Hole

Help me, Lord, I'm
slipping through.
Help me, Lord, I'm
falling.

I'm being pulled in
to a dense black hole
from which there's
no returning.

It's yawning wide;
it's sucking me in,
but there's nothing to see,
it's as black as sin.

Help me, Lord, I'm
sinking down.
Help me,
        Lord,
              I'm
                    drowning . . .

Adrian Rumble

8
7
6
5
4
3
2
1
0
1
2
3
4
5
6
7
8

Prob: BH 99·99%
        NS   0·01%
        Other 0·00%

The Doomed Spaceman

I remember one winter-night meadow
Of sky-black grass
That lay behind my childhood window
Of pearly glass
When I learned what it was to be lonely,
Packed off to bed
And lit by a glimmer that wanly
The frostfall shed.

The pane wiped clear, my crying over,
Darkness would yield
Its long cluster of summer-white clover
In a vast field;
Sleepless I stared for yearning hours,
And I began
Wanting to wander these infinite flowers
When a grown man.

And now I am lost in the heavens,
My meanderings
Further immeasurably flung than Saturn's
Exquisite rings
Into space that's unutterably lovely
With misted light
And every dusk is a dawn and every
Day is as night.

Straight my broken instruments steer:
I have no choice
But to bear silence in which I can hear
No human voice
Save mine at the capsule's clear window
When galaxies pass –
No dandelion Sun in no meadow
Of day-blue grass.

Weightless, helpless, I'm locked on a track
I can't reverse;
For one glimpse of home, I would give back
The universe.
Constellation by constellation
Like baby's breath
I journey through, my destination
Nowhere but Death.

Ted Walker

101

The Ark

This Ark is moving, not on a waste of waters,
But through the bombarding dust of outer space,
Carrying the sole survivors of Earth
On a star trek to a safer place.

Like an echo at an immense distance
From an Earth polluted and scarred by men
Somewhere the twin of Earth orbits a sun
And there perhaps we may begin again.

In the acres of this circular greenhouse
Individual plants and creatures flourish and die;
On the centuries-long voyage through space
They carry life in relays and so do I.

My ancestors escaped in time from Earth
And looking back could see the old home burn;
My descendants will remember their stories
But neither be able nor wish to return.

Generations pass: within this Ark
Prey and predator alike are looking for
That replica planet where, hunted or hunting,
They can begin their life on Earth once more.

Stanley Cook

Towards the Stars

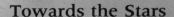

They slept as they set off for the stars
in their refrigerated beds.

They slept as they passed the planets
and headed for outer space.

The stars watched without moving.
Nothing seemed to move anywhere.

They dreamed no dreams
as the stars kept their endless watch.

Then on a fine morning
they opened like blossoms,

they rose still young from their beds
after a hundred years.

Iain Crichton Smith

The swirling world stands still

The swirling world stands still
As I speed on and on
Through aching space
Of stars and light from yesterday.

I cannot tell you why
I make this search. I only know
The ever-hungry asking
Of the human race.

John Kitching

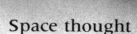

Space thought

Locked in my craft I wonder why
Man has this ceaseless urge to try
To solve the mysteries of space,
When Planet Earth itself's a place
Where problems stare you in the face:
The squabblings of the human race.

Derek Stuart

No need to scan the skies

No need to scan the skies
For what's not known.
The unidentified is here
On earth. The empty space
Of man is unexplained,
Few tunes within his sphere
That other stars would care
To learn to sing.

John Kitching

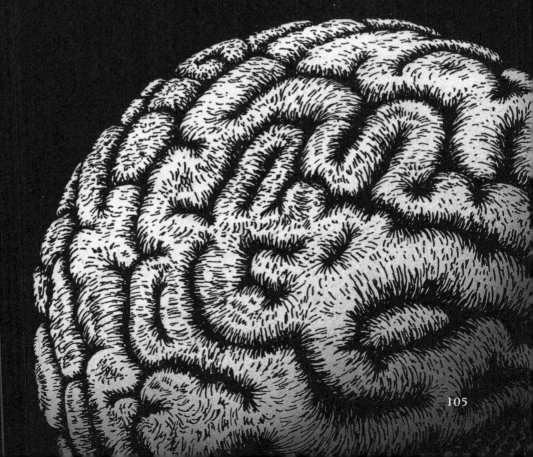

The Astronaut

Star-sailor, with your eyes on space,
You map an ocean in the sky at night.
I see you stride with scientific grace
Upon the crusted suns of yesterday
As if it were tomorrow, in the place
Of time, the voyager beyond this momentary stay
Whose loaded instruments of light
Shoot rocket-galaxies around the bend of sight.

James Kirkup

Retired

He was tired after his voyages,
the shuttles from planet to planet
from star to star.

In the late evening
he would sway in his rocking chair
and watch the moon through the trees.

'I was there once,' he thought
'I stood on that globe.
Now it is like a football
shining in space.'

And he could hardly believe it
that in his helmet
and in his bulky space suit
he'd stirred that far dust.

Iain Crichton Smith

Space Captain

Born poor and known to few,
Sold for a silver song,
Died young, he now rules roosts
Of stars. His arms stretch wide
To welcome home the rest
Of space if we can reach
Beyond the here and now
Of self and yesterday.

John Kitching

Space Walk

A nonsense term. To walk
needs feet with something solid
under, the tug at heel
and toe of gravity,
a firmness for the tensed foot's
arch to grope, grip like a ladder's
rungs under it, and hold,
haul, heave against.

                  Swimming's
not absolutely the word
either, though what you move through
is suffocating ocean
everywhere, a Dead Sea
noiselessly drowning in
a shoreless flood the whole
of Time.

        We step to walk,
of course. But equally
are said to step into the sea.

Raymond Wilson

The Spacefarer (After the Anglo Saxon *The Seafarer*)

This account is true,
In event
And of myself.
Light years of travelling
The darkness
Have left only I,
Writing on dumb screens,
Words too loud to voice.
My thoughts strike
The anvil of silence
And no spark is made.
I cower in the silence
That crashes around me.
I am frightened at my own being
Huddled against controls
That guide the ship
Through seeds and stones of fire
That does not warm me.
No one who has not known it
Can imagine the coldness
Of the absence of a sun.
We found no life
That had shadows
Or could speak to us.
I grieve for my kind,
For landscapes and horizons,
For the lusty life of animals.
I hold myself in my arms,
I drink my tears
Because I cannot bear
To lose them.
The course is set
But will I stay it?
No Being out of its world mould
Can truly know the journey's end.
I sing no more.
I still my hope with my fear,
I still my body
Not to draw the eye of imagined fate.
Will I dare this way again?
My heart misses its wandering beat.

I am bringing the treasured bodies
Of my brothers
Back to their birth planet.
Will the Earth Race
Be at home to us
When I knock?

Julie Holder

The Earth-ling

*Countless years ago the people of Alzorus used the
planet Earth as a lunatic asylum. They called the
people they dumped there 'Earth-lings'.*

I am an earth-ling,
My memory goes back a long way.
I was dumped here long ago.
I lived beneath some overhanging rocks.
Around me at night, through the sky's black sheet,
stars poured down.
It was lonely sitting for centuries
beneath that rain-drenched rock,
wrapped in furs, afraid of this whole terrible planet.
I grew fed up with the taste of its food.
I made fire, I slaughtered creatures,
I walked through a forest and made friends.
I copied the things they made.
I walked through another forest and found enemies,
I destroyed the things they made.
I went on and on and on,
and on a bit more.
I crossed mountains, I crossed new oceans.
I became familiar with this world.
Time would not stop running when I asked it.
I could not whistle for it to come back.
I invented a couple of languages.
I wrote things down.
I invented books.
Time passed.
My inventions piled up. The natives of this planet feared me.
Some tried to destroy me.
Rats came. A great plague swept over the world.
Many of me died.
I am an earth-ling.
I invented cities. I tore them down.
I sat in comfort. I sat in poverty. I sat in boredom.
Home was a planet called Alzorus. A tiny far off star —
One night it went out. It vanished.
I am an earth-ling, exiled for ever from my beginnings.
Time passed. I did things. Time passed. I grew exhausted.

One day
A great fire swept the world.
I wanted to go back to the beginning.
It was impossible.
The rock I had squatted under melted.
Friends became dust,
Dust became the only friend.
In the dust I drew faces of people.
I am putting this message on a feather
and puffing it up among the stars.
I have missed so many things out!
But this is the basic story, the terrible story.
I am an earth-ling,
I was dumped here long ago.
Mistakes were made.

Brian Patten

(This text has been transcribed and translated, using a Titan B78900 computer, from
the Alphan computer printout. This was discovered in the wreckage of a space-vehicle,
which was found in the Himalayas, in 2080.
Only a few fragments of a much longer
document survived the disastrous fire which
destroyed all life-forms on the vehicle.)

Galactic Government Health Warning,
Earth is a high-risk planet,
And is to be visited
Only with the greatest caution.-------------3

MS300Seen through a telescope,
You may think,
Earth a lovely planet.
Alphan travellers are warned,
This is pure deception.
Earth is tricky,
In places, toxic,
And Earth-dwellers
Are not to be trusted,
Being primitive and untamed
Members of the galaxy;
Violent polluters
Of their biosphere.
Earth is as bizarre a planet,
As any in the universe.

Exchanging Data with Earth-men

Earth-men are beginning to learn,
To use computers for communication,
But much data-transfer is done
By a primitive method,
Long-forgotten on Alpha-B 375.
This uses a gaseous medium,
To transmit a pattern
Of low-frequency vibrations,
Over a short distance.
This pattern is coded and decoded,
Into a series of non-digital signals,
Which yet can carry meaning,
When received by head-organs,
Long defunct in Alphans.

You will need several megabytes,
Of computer memory,
To store and decode,
The patterns used,
In addition to
Complex hardware and software.

Earth-men call this system,
SPEECH.

To make matters worse,
Differing patterns are used,
In different parts of Earth.
Earth-men call this system,
LANGUAGE

Being complex, vague, and uncertain,
Many coding and decoding errors
Are produced by these systems,
Earth-men call these errors,
MISUNDERSTANDINGS.

Now you will understand,
Why Earth-men are forever fighting,
Further systems have been observed,
Using sustained vibrations,
At regular intervals,
With repeated patterns,
Some with a mathematical basis.
It is not known why
Earth-men use these.
At times they seem
To have a calming effect,
At other times to excite,
And cause the Earth-men
To move in strange ways,
Even to laugh or weep.
The Earth-men call these systems,
MUSIC and POETRY.

From this you will see,
What a strange planet
Earth can be.

John Cunliffe

115

The Destroyers

Through the spacescope's limitless eyes
See far below us that charred star
That is the planet Earth, or was
The planet Earth before
Those who once inhabited it
Destroyed it.

        The destroyers
Began as seeds sown by us when
Aeons ago –
Meaningless word to us
Who live outside of time –
Our space seekers found what was then
A cooling world ready to receive
The gift of life.

        We monitored that world.
Remembering our blanched barren home
Surrounded by black space,
Watched with mounting envy
The oceans' myriad azures,
The lovely land mantled
With myriad greens and fragile flowers,
Creatures without number,
And, mastering them,
That strange forked being
Who finally destroyed what it
Had mastered and been given
To hold in trust.

We came
To intervene, we knew
What might happen. We miscalculated.
The suddenness of the final catastrophe
Caught us unawares. So much for
Our vaunted wisdom,
Our all-powerful mind.

Let us
Take one final look, recalling
That unimaginable beauty.
In time Earth will renew herself.
We will come again
In another aeon
And sow the seed once more.

Albert Rowe

The Choice

They were landing and the great thrust
Pressed like magnetism on their bodies.
The great ship hovered then slowly
Dropped on meadow grass.

Starglyn, the captain, stared
At the green landscape.
Between two hills a deserted city,
Crumbling and overgrown, patterned
The Scanning Screen. The dials
On a Blue Screen indicated
No human life present.

Suncon, the Celestial Geologist,
Smiled over his captain's shoulder.

'You were right' said Starglyn.
'They must have been a very aggressive people.
What was your main source of information?'

'The great meteorite which broke
From Earth in 2048 A.D.
We took it to Station Z
And examined it. It told us everything.'

'What?' asked Starglyn.

'They were allowed to choose
Between good and evil.
And they chose evil . . .'

'Bloody fools' muttered Starglyn.

Robert Morgan

'Do you think we'll ever get to see Earth, sir?'

I hear they're hoping to run trips
one day, for the young and fit, of course.
I don't see much use in it myself;
there'll be any number of places
you can't land, because they're still toxic,
and even in the relatively safe bits
you won't see what it was; what it could be.
I can't fancy a tour through the ruins
of my home with a party of twenty-five
and a guide to tell me what to see.
But if you should see some beautiful thing,
some leaf, say, damascened with frost,
some iridescence on a pigeon's neck,
some stone, some curve, some clear water;
look at it as if you were made of eyes,
as if you were nothing but an eye, lidless
and tender, to be probed and scorched
by extreme light. Look at it with your skin,
with the small hairs on the back of your neck.
If it is well-shaped, look at it with your hands;
if it has fragrance, breathe it into yourself;
if it tastes sweet, put your tongue to it.
Look at it as a happening, a moment;
let nothing of it go unrecorded,
map it as if it were already passing.
Look at it with the inside of your head,
look at it for later, look at it for ever,
and look at it once for me.

Sheenagh Pugh

The Beautiful Strangers

(after sighting an Unidentified Flying Object)

They are above us,
Beyond us and around us,
Out of space out of time.

Between star and star,
New moons, and beings wiser
Than ourselves, approach.

Our earth is rotten
As fruit about to drop
Into nothingness.

They are gardeners
Of space, who come to tend us.
Strangers, they love us.

Strangers, they love us.

In ages long past
They came to our planet.
We drove them away.

Ever since that day
Our world moves to destruction.
Death grows among us.

Only if we call
To the beautiful strangers
Will our peace return.

I know they watch me
As I write this poem now.
Poets are cosmic.

I feel their silence
Like words, their absence like love.
I belong not to this earth.

I belong to them, and they
Are my brothers, their space my home
That is not of this earth.

Ever a stranger, I came
From further fields, an outer place
Whose clouds I trail to death.

Ever a white shadow wandering
On this lost world, white and alone
Among the crowding shades of black,

My one voice cries to you, men
Of earth, out of my solitude,
That we must turn to them.

We must watch for them.
We must give our hearts and souls,
Open eyes and arms.

Look to the heavens
And upon the ground for signs.
They are among us as I am among you.

And we shall see them
With the eyes of vision, if
We have sense to see.

And we shall know them
By their purity and grace,
If we have hearts to feel.

Where are my lost brothers?
Let them come back to me!
Let us return to them!

They are above us,
Beyond us and around us,
Out of space out of time.

James Kirkup

Optics

The earth from a distance
seems clearer by far
than peering at insects
locked in a jam-jar.

Binocular landscape
at 5 mile range
is etched in sharp detail
and set beyond change.

To observe from a mountain
or cumulus sky
gives the sacred proportion
to God's only eye.

Likewise the past
viewed from present terrain
reshuffles confusion
and makes patterns plain.

Such far-off soil
still filters my blood:
sight leaps through lenses
avoiding the flood.

I'm part of that country
locked into my sight;
its soil made my eyes
look back on its light.

Near speaks to far
and far answers near,
harmony forming
and meaning more clear.

Between the unseen and seen
mind's optics descend,
machine of perception
in space without end.

Alan Sillitoe

In the late evening

In the late evening
they approached Earth.
It winked like a tiny diamond.

It seemed too small to land on
after gaunt Neptune
after shadowy Jupiter.

And then they remembered.
This was the only planet
not named after a god.

It seemed so small so unimportant
And yet their hearts trembled
more crazily than their needles.

Iain Crichton Smith

Ballad of the Sad Astronaut

Why are you weeping, child of the future,
For what are you grieving, son of the earth?
Acorns of autumn and white woods of winter,
Song-thrush of spring in the land of my birth.

You have a new life, child of the future,
Drifting through stars to a land of your own.
With Sirius to guide you, Orion beside you
Wandering the heavens you are free from earth's harm.

I have a new life, the speckled skies' beauty,
Left far behind me the dark cries of earth;
Oh, but I long for the soft rains of April,
Ice-ferned Decembers and suns of the south.

What was I dreaming, to drift with Orion,
To leave for cold Neptune my home and my hearth?
Stars in their millions stretch endless, remind me
Far far behind lies my blue-marbled earth.

Here on the hillside the dawn is just rising,
Buttercups dew-fill, all silken and gold.
Well may you weep, sad child of the future,
Well may you yearn for your beautiful world.

Judith Nicholls

Index of Titles and First Lines

First lines are shown in italic.

Acknowledgements

The following poems are appearing for the first time in this collection and are reprinted by permission of the author unless otherwise stated.

Leo Aylen: 'The Undistinguished Visitor'. Copyright © 1985 by Leo Aylen.   Alan Bold: 'Stars', 'Moon', 'Last Men on Mars', 'The Tenth Planet'. All Copyright © 1985 by Alan Bold   Charles Connell: 'Space Men'. Copyright © 1985 by Charles Connell.   Stanley Cook: 'The Launch', 'Apollo', 'Man on Moon', 'The Ark'. All Copyright © 1985 by Stanley Cook.   John Cunliffe: 'Alpha-B375-Earth Visitors Guide'. Copyright © 1985 by John Cunliffe.   Iain Crichton-Smith: 'The Children', 'Strangers', 'Towards the Stars', 'Retired', 'In the Late Evening'. All Copyright © 1985 by Iain Crichton-Smith.   Eric Finney: 'Our Solar System'. Copyright © 1985 by Eric Finney.   Pamela Gillilan: 'Alien Goes Shopping', 'Alien at the Zoo'. Both Copyright © 1985 by Pamela Gillilan.   David Harmer: 'The Space Explorer's Story'. Copyright © 1985 by David Harmer.   Neil Harries: 'Dog-Watch'. Copyright © 1985 by Neil Harries.   Julie Holder: 'Four Children, One being', 'The Spacefarer', 'Space Joke', 'Count Down'. All Copyright © 1985 by Julie Holder. Jean Kenward: 'Sun', 'Moon', 'Moon', 'Planets', 'What's Out There?', 'E.T.'. All Copyright © 1985 by Jean Kenward.   James Kirkup: 'Space Trip', 'My Thing from Outer Space', 'Questions and Answers'. All Copyright © 1985 by James Kirkup.   John Kitching: 'The Planets Turn in Stately Dance', 'Within the Space', 'I Know Where I'm Going', 'If He Cried, He Cried in Private', 'The Swirling World Stands Still', 'No Need to Scan the Skies', 'Space Captain'. All Copyright © 1985 by John Kitching.   Roger McGough: 'Phew'. Copyright © 1985 by Roger McGough. Reprinted by permission of A. D. Peters & Co., Ltd.   Wes Magee: 'The Fungus Fingers', 'Epitaphs for Some Space Beasts'. Both Copyright © 1985 by Wes Magee.   Judith Nicholls: 'Watch This Space', 'Andromeda', 'Moonscape', 'Earthset Earthrise', 'Space-Shuttle', 'Ballad of the Sad Astronaut'. All Copyright © 1985 by Judith Nicholls.   John Rice: 'I am . . . star Counting', 'Sky Season', 'Sun Stuff', 'Brokendown Countdown', 'Man and Height', 'Rockets and Quasars', 'On Some Other Planet'. All Copyright © 1985 by John Rice.   Michael Rosen: 'Aldrin Collins and Armstrong', 'Here is the News from Space', 'Humpty Dumpty Went to the Moon'. All Copyright © 1985 by Michael Rosen.   Albert Rowe: 'Space Settlement', 'The Destroyers'. Both copyright © 1985 by Albert Rowe.   Adrian Rumble: 'The Eagle has Landed', 'A Close Encounter', 'Unique?', 'Black Hole'. All Copyright © 1985 by Adrian Rumble.   Derek Stuart: 'The Space Race', 'Save our Spaceship', 'Space Thought'. All Copyright © 1985 by Derek Stuart.   Jenny Thomas: 'Space'. Copyright © Jenny Thomas 1985.   Ted Walker: 'The Doomed Spaceman'. Reprinted by permission of David Higham Associates Ltd.   Raymond Wilson: 'Davy by Starlight', 'Never Since Eden', 'Space Walk'. All Copyright © 1985 by Raymond Wilson.

The Editor and Publisher wish to thank the following for permission to reprint copyright poems in this anthology.

Jack Bevan: 'To the Moon' from Salvatore Quasimodo, Collected Poems, translated by Jack Bevan (Anvil Press). By permission of the author.   Max Boyce: 'The ballad of Morgan the Moon' from I Was There. Reprinted by permission of George Weidenfeld and Nicolson Ltd.   Max Fatchen: '' Jump over the Moon?' the cow declared . . .'' and 'Space Shot' from Songs for my dog & Other People (Kestrel Books 1980), pp. 30, 63, Copyright © 1980 by Max Fatchen. Reprinted by permission of Penguin Books Ltd., and John Johnson/Winant Towers Ltd.   Ted Hughes: 'Moon-Wind' from Moon bells and Other Poems (Publ. by Chatto & Windus) and 'Moon-transport' from The Earth Owl & Other Moon-People. Published in the US in Moon-Whales & Other Moon People (Viking Penguin Inc.) © 1963, 1976, by Ted Hughes. Reprinted by permission of Faber and Faber Ltd., and Viking Penguin Inc.   Adrian Mitchell: 'Song in Space', from Nothingmas Day. Reprinted by permission of Allison and Busby Ltd.   John Travers Moore: 'Astronauts' from There's Motion Everywhere. Copyright 1970 by John Travers Moore. (Houghton Mifflin Company). Reprinted by permission of the author.   Edwin Morgan: 'The First Men on Mercury', 'Spacepoem 3: Off Course'. Copyright Edwin Morgan, from Poems of Thirty Years, Carcanet, Manchester 1982. Reprinted by permission of the Publisher.   Robert Morgan: 'The Choice' from Frontiers of Living (ed. John Fairfax). Reprinted by permission of Granada Publishing Ltd.   Norman Nicholson: 'Off to Outer Space Tomorrow Morning' © Norman Nicholson 1984. Reprinted from The Candy-floss Tree: Poems by Gerda Mayer, Frank Flynn, and Norman Nicholson (1984) by permission of Oxford University Press.   Gareth Owen: 'Make Believe', 'Shed in Space', 'Space Shot', 'The Owl and the Astronaut' and 'Message Understood' from Song of the City. Reprinted by permission of Fontana Paperbacks.   Brian Patten: 'The Earthling' from Gangsters, Ghosts and Dragonflies. Reprinted by permission of Anthony Sheil Associates Ltd.   Sheenagh Pugh: 'The Craft I Left in was called Esau', 'Do you think We'll get to see Earth, Sir?'. Both from Earth Studies and Other Voyages. Reprinted by permission of the Poetry Wales Press, for the author.   R. C. Scriven: 'The Marrog' from Journeys (Spring 1968). Reprinted by permission of the author.   Alan Sillitoe: 'Optics' from Sun Before Departure (Granada, 1984). By permission of the author.   Geoffrey Summerfield: 'Sci-Fi Horrorscopes' from Welcome and Other Poems. Reprinted by permission of Andre Deutsch, for the author.